The Map of Unseen Things

by

Brett Warren

Pine Row Press

for all
who find themselves
in unseen territories

The Map of Unseen Things

Published by Pine Row Press
Ft. Mitchell, KY 41011

ISBN: 978-1-7363394-9-7

February 2023

First Edition

10 9 8 7 6 5 4 3 2 1

=====

Poet's website at brettwarrenpoetry.com

Author photo: John S. Parke

Publisher's website at pinerow.com

Publication Acknowledgments

Grateful acknowledgments to the editors of publications in which the following poems have appeared, sometimes in earlier versions:

Canary: "Mouse Log"

Cape Cod & the Islands Magazine: "Extra Terrestrial," "Synapse"

Cape Cod Poetry Review: "Still Life with Skeletons and Asian Pear"

The Comstock Review: "The Apartment"

duality: "Erasure," "Infinity," "*Sub rosa*"

Eunoia Review: "My Father-in-Law Arrives for the Last Time," "Triangle"

Green Fuse: "Mourning Dove"

Halfway Down the Stairs: "A Daughter Is Clearing Out the House Next Door," "L'chaim"

Harbor Review: "The Agnostic's Rapture"

Hole in the Head Review: "Learning to Fly," "Mothers of Boys," "Science & Religion @ 5 am," "Suicide Rosary," "Topaz"

ONE ART: "Origami of Shock"

One Sentence Poems: "If I'm Lucky," "Mooncake in a Chinese Bakery"

Pine Row Journal: "The Hawk Elizabeth," "Helen"

Provincetown Magazine: "Mistakes of Attraction"

Right Hand Pointing: "After I Faint on Easter," "The Artist at 90"

Shot Glass Journal: "Feral Muse," "Word"

Turtle Island Quarterly: "More"

The Westchester Review: "Trompe l'oeil on the Capital Beltway"

Contents

Three

Four

Five

The Map of Unseen Things

A map of the world
that does not include Utopia
is not worth even glancing at.
—Oscar Wilde

One

Second Sight

The story goes they raced toward midnight
to the hospital on a hill overlooking Seattle.
A wind came in from the northwest.

It was fifty-five degrees—cool for August,
a relief to someone as pregnant as she was.
I imagine their mood was festive.

In the parking lot, he sped to the end
of a row, ran around the car to help her
onto the spongy grass. As she stood,

her knitting bag toppled and everything
spilled out. Balls of color rolled in all directions.
He would have let them go. But even with me

simmering inside her, she made him gather yarn
while she leaned against the car, laughing.
Maybe her hair was tied back with a ribbon.

Maybe it fell loose around her shoulders.
She loved to tell this story. Some search
for a defining moment, the stirrings of trouble

in trauma or loss, or something lurking
in the deep end of the gene pool.
But maybe it's just the fact of being born

into a particular story, chained to its fate
as the last tumbler drops into place, a lock
that will take decades to break. The sky

was cloudy. She couldn't have seen the moon—
only the silent lights of the parking lot. She stood,
breathing temperate air, breathing the change

becoming real. Everything still seemed perfect.
If I could, I would thank her for the gift
of stopping time before I arrived.

Myriapod

From the other room, I heard her tell him
how that morning I'd come running
with my cigar box of broken crayons
to show her a centipede I'd found there.
She carried the box outside, set it down
on the lawn, its lid open wide, ran back inside.
I about died! she said, and they laughed.
They were having drinks. She was at the stove
making dinner. He leaned against the counter,
the way he always did, necktie loosened,
briefcase slouching on the yellow step-stool
by the back door. The sun began to disappear,
and I thought I could hear, beyond the rattle-
music of ice in a glass, the segmented surprise
coming into its time in the darkening grass,
the first danger I ever loved.

Divination with Chicken Guts

Giblets came in a bloody packet
for my mom to unwrap
and cook for the cat.
She'd set them in a corner
of the roasting pan
where the bird lay headless
on her back, bereft of feathers
and modesty. One time
she found two hearts,
held them shining
in her palm, as if to say
you and me. As if she knew
it had always been,
would always be
the two of us,
before any beginning,
after any end.
I was born knowing
what she was born knowing.
I could see my heart
in the hen's heart,
my ribcage identical
to hers, the innards
not hidden in sodden paper
but suspended in a cavern
of curved bones.
I already knew something
of what else was inside—
how expansive it was,
how starry and dark.

After I Faint on Easter

my mom hauls me
down to the basement

of my grandparents' church,
presses a wet paper towel

to my face   mutters
goddamn fire & brimstone

having left small-town religion
for a salvation of her own.

In the pews, those who stayed
whisper *black sheep, black lamb.*

Helen

I can hardly stand to tell you
how when my dad was a boy,
his father put their cat, whose name
was Helen, into a burlap sack
with her kittens and some rocks
and threw them into the Columbia River.
If you've ever stood on its banks,
you know how it runs dark gray-green
below the Angel's Rest, how it rolls
and churns and twists along the Gorge,
where hemlocks and blackjack pines
bear witness, and clouds press down
like a shroud. But now that you know,

I can tell you how when I was a girl
in California, the cat we named Muffy
had kittens not once but twice: the first litter
born too early, hairless and stillborn
under the ferns, the next a spirited gang
of five. I can tell you how their eyes
opened like stars coming out at night.
How fearlessly they climbed,
our curtains pocked with snags
forever after. How they fanned out
around a saucer to wean themselves,
stubby tails sticking out like rays,
the way I used to draw the sun.

I knew nothing of Helen then.
But when the kitten-gang had gone,

we watched as Muffy's spay-incision
twisted and swelled from angry red
to pink to paler still, finally smoothing
into scar—a marvel, how damage
can undo itself to something new.
May it be so with all the old
unspoken wounds.

Smitty

I can still see her on her knees,
with gloves and white vinegar,
swearing and scrubbing
where our silver tabby had marked
the dark-green swivel chair
        in the back, where I wouldn't know
        till it was goddamn dry.
The week before it was the pocket door,
before that the front of the stereo speaker,
black fabric soaked to the paper cone inside—
        really left his mark this time!

But she'd always had a weakness
for the handsome and the bad.
The dreamy cad they called Red
who made the girls in high school swoon.
Yul Brynner with his shaved head,
arms folded across his bare chest.
And her first husband—a cheater—
a story she finally told over margaritas
when she was 70 years old.
        Black Irish, she said,
        with blue eyes like glass.

The house was chaos anyway—
it just seemed easier to let Smitty stay,
even with the attacks on our other cat.
One Christmas Eve he chased her
room to room and up the tree,
which crashed to the floor, confetti bomb

of colored lights and ornament glass.
She rummaged through the junk drawer,
found a piece of string to lash the trunk
to something steady, because Smitty
was *a thing of beauty,*
if not a joy forever.

How to Save a Girl

in memory of my dad

Kids deserve the right to think that they
can change the world. —Lois Lowry

let her make a nest under the stairs
with books and old bedding
paper flowers and peace signs
and when she learns about the war
let her hang the flag upside down

let her choose the dog on his last day
at the pound   let her be the one
to name him

let them set off through rubbled fields
and ruined creeks
trust the dog to come and go
listening and listening in the losing
and finding

let her learn the languages that matter
salamander   mouse   millipede
snake

let her be quiet

and when the household erupts
let the dog and the girl find refuge
on the other side of a closed door

or let them disappear in a stand of trees
trust her to know   like a bird
where to go

Sub rosa

I fell in for a time with some sixth-grade girls
who smuggled an eye-shadow paintbox to school.
I was the mule. We met in the girls' room
to admire the package, its innocent design—

like us, it held something daring inside.
We perched on sinks to pass the contraband
hand to hand, sharing the single stunted brush.
The best color, we thought, was powder blue.

Lay it on thick! we said. Because what's the point
if no one sees your signal flag? But waving
isn't planting when *esprit de corps* is the thing.
So we lined up again in front of the mirror,

white paper towels our conditional surrender,
and rubbed our lids pink at the end of the day.

Erasure

The irony is not lost on 12-year-old girls
who sit in chairs that are welded to desks
and slouch or fidget while being erased
two afternoons a week   by an unmarried
greasy-haired pimply-faced Home Ec teacher
who lectures intrusively on personal hygiene
skin-care regimens   and the double-shampoo
because a girl should always look her best.

Meanwhile across the hall   the boys
are in shop class   being erased
by a self-appointed father figure
who picks on *punks* and *sissies* and *jockstraps*
and barks orders at those who struggle
to make birdhouses of scrap wood
or heat-fuse bits of acrylic into tri-colored
promise rings.

A girl might be lucky enough to get one
if she loiters fetchingly in deafening tunnels
where dangling padlocks and slamming lockers
are symbols in a rehearsal
for *the most important time of a girl's life.*

They never taught us to balance a checkbook
pay bills   get a job   or negotiate anything
but I did learn to make *petits fours*
for the ladies' teas I would never host

and lollipops for the children
I would choose not to have.

No thank you   I said in my 12-year-old head
no thanks.

Word

Someone has spray-painted the word *DIE*
on the pavement where the road
snakes through swaying reeds, away
from the beach, back toward town.
The word is red. I stand where he stood,
imagining the thin arms of a boy,
his determined finger on the nozzle,
the nascent muscles of his back
and his perfect pink guts all knotted up.
It’s as dark outside as it is in
when he bends forward, doubled over
by his small crime, the act of one
too young to know the word he chose
is an empty threat. Soon the men from town
will roll up in their rattling, dripping truck,
get out their buckets and long-handled rollers,
teach him what to do with pain.

Koi

The white boys stream in,
synchronized, fanatical,
always having to be first,

passing as a single shadow
below the footbridge
to coveted water near the rock

where I stand. They want me
to feed them, their mouths
gaping like discarded condoms.

Their fervor sends a charge
through the water, fevers
the other fish like hysteria

or a virus, until they become
a nameless churning thing
made of nameless churning

things. One ancient fish
with black and yellow scales
and a tattered tail

turns and turns on the edge
of the gathering storm,
a windsock anchored by age.

Another fish, smaller
and splotched with early orange,
waits in the shallows,

a ghastly cauliflower
growing from his head.
The rest push in again

and again, and some
hoist themselves halfway
onto flat rocks, unafraid,

willing to risk the deadly air.
Others half-heartedly try,
get jostled and slapped

in a crush of muscled sides.
Thirteen is the age
for testing the ledge,

for leaning toward danger.
The damp and suffocating air
presses at my back,

a churning suspicion
that I too am full
of nameless things,

the pond a prophecy, a mirror,
my heart a floating prize
that lodges in my throat.

Fight or Flight

No one ever talked about the storms,
the slamming doors, the station wagon
that teetered and swung like a tornado
around blind curves in the road.

The three of them always at each other,
a throwing star that crackled the air
with sky-to-ground lightning.
They only told stories

that could be made to sound funny.
Piles of dirty clothes hurled
from a second-floor window
to flutter down across the lawn.

Suitcase splayed across a bed
until someone grabbed it by the handle
in a crack-the-whip flip, and then
everything flying. Vinyl record

ripped from the turntable mid-song
to be snapped in half. Jumbo bottle
of Jean Naté smashed in the upstairs tub,
the house reeking for weeks.

But the most spectacular storm
touched down in the kitchen
one morning before school—
my mom in a half-pivot between

the dishwasher's dropped jaw
and the cupboards' wide-
open eyes when a sudden drop
in barometric pressure

raised her arms like a funnel cloud
and sent a stack of dinner plates
crashing to the floor and the dog
scrabbling to get under the table

and cats scattering in all directions,
tails puffed out like bottle brushes.
And that, they liked to say,
is how we got new dishes!

But the story I want to tell is the one
about the day after I left home.
I awakened in a narrow bed
I'd pushed under the open window

the night before   and the first thing I saw
was the sky of my own life   all blue
except for clouds so faint   so far away I knew

they had no meaning   other than altitude.

Two

Mothers of Boys

One frosted her hair.
It might have been a wig.
She enjoyed an afternoon martini,
toy poodles arranged
like sofa pillows around her.
She didn't bother to get up.

Two had a head injury
from a car accident
six months before her wedding,
which went forward anyway
out of duty. People said
her husband was *burdened,*
a *saint*, and she was *shrill.*
But I liked the way
she snapped her gum
and stood in the front yard
brandishing a cooking spoon
at speeders.

Three was divorced,
and had to work
as a hostess in a restaurant.
She had black hair
halfway down her back,
black boots up
to her knees.
She had seen it all
and she was tired.
When she talked,

a cigarette bobbed
in the corner of her mouth,
and when she stopped,
it dangled there.
If ashes dropped to the floor,
they were ignored.

Four was always
wiping down countertops.
She was the wife
of an alcoholic.

Five was nervous.
She confided once
when we were alone
that she had *diverticulitis.*
I pretended I knew
what that was.
She was married
to a demolitions expert.

Six kept a crucifix in every room
and a squirt bottle of holy water
on the sill by the kitchen sink.
I wasn't Catholic. I thought
it was sin repellent.

I never met Seven. I left for college,
which turned out to be a fast track
to freedom. But I swore
I could feel her suburban curses
rise up and catch a tailwind

from middle America
all the way to the coast,

where I was already learning
all the ways women find
to say no, how sometimes
it becomes an affirmation.

Topaz

Though I know exactly where you are,
and it's not far, it seems unlikely
we'll see each other again. We lived
in a rented house with a kitchen so small
there wasn't room to change your mind.
Or so you said. But you made sourdough bread
in the creaky oven, omelets in a hinged pan
you could snap shut and flip over an open flame.
You grew catnip in a pot on the porch,
and the cat curled around it to nap in the sun.
We smoked into the night, again in the morning.
Once you spilled the bong on the carpet.
We never did get the smell out. We were young.
I'm not sure we really tried. The garage had doors
nailed together by someone before our time,
scrap wood painted over but still rotten
from the bottom, a hole big enough for a cat
to squeeze through. Ours stood half in, half out
of it the morning after she was hit by a car,
made it home but had to be put down anyway.
I sold my motorbike to pay the bill. I went back
a few years ago, crawled along in my rental car
past the corner store where we walked
to buy a single bottle of beer. The house
was gone, torn down to build something new.
Your eyes were topaz. Strangers in churches
always thought you were the savior.
You've taken yourself away from everyone
who knew you then. Sometimes one of them

remembers something, wonders where you are.
I don’t tell. One thing I know is that you
don’t want to be found.

The Apartment

We packed on separate days,
careful not to disturb each other,
a consideration we hadn't shown
for months, a kindness reserved
for ghosts.

The pictures came down one by one,
bleaching the walls.
I flipped through record albums—
yours, mine, yours, mine—
a few I couldn't remember
whose they were, we'd had them
so long. I left those for you.
As small as a child's, the bronze hand
you made in casting class rested tenderly,
palm up, on the windowsill near my desk,
a gift again.

On the days you were at work
I walked room to room
to see what you'd done during the night.
The rooms took sides. Your boxes stood
neat as soldiers against one wall,
my belongings slouched
against the other. Neither of us
took everything all at once:
a load of yours, a load of mine.
You finished first, left your keys
on the counter. When I went back
the last night, the emptiness

felt bigger than our life together.
The light from the streetlamp
slipped in and lay defeated
on the floor, undisturbed
by even the sound of a clock ticking.

Mistakes of Attraction

I awaken to the tinny metronome of a bee
bumping against the second-floor screen
to get at a vase of flowers on the sill.
I think of us again. I know what it is
to fly all the way up into the trees
for nothing.

I uncover the patio furniture, find corpses
strewn across flowered cushions—
insects who lusted for pollen
but suffocated under plastic skies.

Everywhere I look, reminders.
A swallowtail teeters among sagging petals
while the cat watches from the porch.
A mantis prays for romance, even though
he's about to lose his head.

I wonder if you remember
the mouse we found electrocuted
when we pulled the old stove
away from the wall—a crinkle of gray fur
in an outlet box, which must have seemed
the perfect place to stay warm.

Mourning Dove

So this is how it ends: one last phone call,
an informing note—a thunderclap on glass,
a quiver of feathers, a head thrust into snow.
Hoping she is only stunned, I jam on my boots
and run outside, around the house,
struggling through iron snow
in the rounding madness of a dream
where you can't move fast enough
and the corners keep coming and coming.

But when I reach her, scoop her up,
her neck is limp as string, her spinal cord
released from the intricate clasp of tendon
and bone. A splurge of blood lacquers her beak,
a poison-tipped arrow. Pearl frost covers her eyes.
I see her as she is and was, her truth
and detail, and lay the dove on a dark rock
that offers itself from beneath the snow.

On the window, her ghost floats,
imprinted in powder down: twisted beak
that smacked into nothingness,
tilted eye that finally recognized
the illusions of the other side—
perpetual flowers on sofa and rug,
painted birds in a frame on the wall.
What am I to make of this wrongful death,
the spherical stamp of her breast,
the outline of her wings—like yours—
extended in hard flight, feather tips reaching
for the reckless pitch of terminal velocity?

Suicide Rosary

For years I thought of it as a rosary,
every bead a different color. Milky
white of the coroner's nocturnal skin,
his waxy hands clutching a clipboard.
Red-brown spatters of blood on the wall.
Amber pooled in a shot glass squatting
on the nightstand, yellow label
of the tequila bottle standing at its side.
Lapis blue jeans, crumpled the way they do
when they fall to the floor and someone
crawls into bed for the last time.

But I've put the rosary aside to tell you
that the police radio was what woke me,
and strange lights flashing without a sound.
That every night at 3 a.m., I was jolted awake
by a gunshot I can't remember hearing.
That this went on for more than a year,
and all I could do was stare at the ceiling,
because I had nowhere to go with my grief,
my rage, questions I couldn't even frame.
That I was afraid this would happen
every night for the rest of my life.

But time, in its time, brought the surprise
of morning light through naked glass. The sun
on more than one day. I won't lie and say
I don't remember, don't think of it, if it
happens to be 3 a.m. and I'm awakened
by beginning rain or the slamming car door

of the neighbors' drunken son. But memory
isn't a bullet in my brain. It's not a rosary.
If I say healing isn't being made whole,
I might mean peace is a string that frays
until it breaks, and the beads just fall.

Pariah Dog

I know the type because of you—pariah dog
who lives on the edge, prowling for food
or a bone to chew, guarding it tooth and growl
until something better comes along. I was sixteen,
primed for heartbreak, and you delivered.
But how you dazzled with all that swagger
and lean muscle, those blinding teeth
in flawless scissor-jaws like some Egyptian god.
I see you achieved biological success: married
(more than once), even managed to propagate
the genes a few times. But now you live alone
in a mobile home that goes nowhere, set down
in a diorama of discarded things: rusty parts,
deflated balls, motors that just won't start
or sputter out after a minute or two.
You get your dinner from a grubby microwave
that squats like Anubis in the shadow of pyramids
made of beer cans on the countertop, and flop
into a recliner with a broken handle, your sagging face
not so handsome anymore. If you remember
how you used to say *love 'em and leave 'em*,
if you think back on your glory days, I'm pretty sure
it's not the same way some of us do. But it's okay.
Do you even know what *schadenfreude* is?
Never mind. I can afford to be kind. Let's just say
you look a little *basic* compared to how you were
before, and close the door.

Learning to Fly

After the rape, I took up
with a paraplegic guy
who said he'd gotten high
and jumped off a building,
thinking he could fly.
I wasn't convinced this
was what really happened.
But his story seemed important,
the kind of truth that might arise
when you're trying to survive.
We slept on his waterbed,
which was tidal and complicated,
but also peaceful, like when
the wheels of a plane lift off
and you get to be nowhere,
in between places for a while.
We were both damaged.
He had learned to adapt.
I was new to it, noticing
obstacles everywhere. Curbs.
Stairs. Doors that swung out
instead of in. He had to look up
at the liquor-store clerk,
who had to look down
at him. He kept his money
in a canvas bag, its handles
slung over the back of his chair.
He'd ask the clerk, or even
a stranger, to fish his wallet
out, shimmy a six-pack in.

The bottles rattled
when he crossed
the threshold and rolled
down the uneven sidewalk.
He wore racing gloves,
the kind with no fingers,
so he could save his hands.
Sometimes I'd sit on his lap
and we'd tear down
the dark streets
of our college town,
flashing in and out
of pools of light,
past ruined lawns
and palatial houses
where frat boys
passed out drunk
on top of their victims,
no one awake
to see us flying by.

Visitation by an Almost-Famous Actor

I always knew it was you, leaving tabloid stories
taped to my door—running gags that fluttered

like prayer flags: "Woman with Four Legs
Opens Dance Studio," "UFO Turns Back, Horrified,"

"Man Enters Elevator, Disappears"—and the echo
of your presence, a rush of knowing only time

separated us. Your shoes on this concrete.
Your palm on this railing. Your fingers

on the surface of this door. Now, even before
you appear, I recognize certain dreams as yours.

It's midnight. I cross a side street toward a black car,
keys in hand, but detour into a Mexican restaurant—

you know the place: high ceilings, tall windows,
terra cotta floor. Your best friend stands

under a spotlight, holding a box overflowing
with photographs. You with arms flung wide

at the end of a song. You wearing circus tights
or a vintage suit or a bird costume. You with some dog

you'd taken in, always the oldest or ugliest, always
a torn curtain or cracked window in the background.

A crowd presses the stage, star-struck.
Asleep or awake, I'm still stuck

on how diminished the world seems without you.
I make my way through a maze of rickety chairs

to a swinging door, and there you are, a waiter this time,
your eyes like broken china, your tuxedo a size too small.

You're older, gray   the way I never got to see you.
You're waiting for an order to come up,

just here for a walk-on   like before.
You know you're dead, but didn't you always?

I rest my hand on a tabletop that looks like ice
and feels like cool water. Our fingers almost touch,

and I remember, again: all that separates us
is time, just an ordinary piece of glass.

The air shimmers with masa harina
and old epiphanies that still intoxicate. I say

I miss you   *and without opening your mouth*
you say   I know.

Three

L'chaim
("to life")

It felt like hate   every time I passed by
charred cotton-candy branches
where my father went tree to tree
in the yard   reached up with a click-lighter
to set caterpillar nests on fire.

I renamed it anger   at circumstance
at life   at how he'd landed so far
from who he'd always been.
When a bird fell down his chimney
righted itself   perched on the grate
eyes bright as onyx beads
he couldn't figure out what to do
so he beat it to death with a brass-
handled fireplace poker.

If he had called me
I would have come with my net.

Whatever I named it   whatever the cause
in a corner of my heart   I carried
and could not forgive   the wound
a sickness   that he would take
from the world   these living things.

But I began to heal   the night
we were packing for his last move
and a black mouse lit out
across the stained carpeting

like a fuse along the baseboard.
I had found and destroyed
the glue traps   months ago.
I struggled to suppress a laugh
in the back of my throat

and stayed where I was   kneeling
among papers and boxes
while something flickered
at the corners of my mouth
and branched out
with a giddy crackling
like a tree on fire.

Origami of Shock

The first time was the worst: how graciously
he opened the door to welcome me in,

saying I had just missed them—the figurines
who like to run back and forth across the carpet.

How he made a little running motion
with his fingers, adding that if I'd come earlier,
I'd have seen a tiny version of myself

perched on the bookshelf among knick-knacks
and a fine layer of dust. How his eyes
kept darting over to see if I/she was still there.

How a life-sized version of me began to edge
toward the door, feeling my way along the wall
with my shoulder.

How I couldn't take my eyes off him,
couldn't break free from the terrible trance
of his smile. How the thing

that brought me back was my left hand,
which had been in my coat pocket

the whole time, folding a grocery list
into smaller and smaller squares.

Still Life with Skeletons and Asian Pear

I

At the beginning of each week,
I sit with her and make up reasons
it's not a good week to die:
a ride in the car, her favorite dinner planned.
Lately my reasons have become ridiculous.
I've finally hired a court jester.
The queen is giving you a medal.
On Thursday we'll make a birthday cake
and set it on fire. She can't understand
the words anymore—it's the telling
she hears. This I believe without evidence.

II

Outside, wind sweeps water
onto the beach. It rings the rope
against the flagpole, like a temple bell
or the singular note of someone sobbing.
We spend an hour preparing to go.
I hear the wind dying down.
She insists on carrying a black vinyl purse
that snaps open and shut with its brassy tooth.
On the sand, dozens of baby horseshoe crabs
have washed up, each parchment exoskeleton
a perfect miniature of its parent, but translucent.
She pauses, wondering or remembering.
I pace back and forth between the dead babies
and the old lady in the sequined hat.

III

I try to let go of the need to understand.
She is like an Asian pear or a tapestry,
a gold glaze the modern world
could never replicate. I see the precision
of this color and everything within it.
When I close my eyes, I can see it as clearly
as I can hear the rising and falling of her breath.
I am afraid of forgetting her the way she was.
None of us will survive THIS,
she says, frowning at her dinner plate.
I fall asleep on the sofa, and in my dream
I am standing on a bridge
with the ghost of my actor friend.
He walks along the railing and says,
You have to let go of letting go.
He thinks this is funny,
extremely obvious. I wake up.
Everything seems steady, absolute.
I begin to practice remembering.

The Artist at 90

In the Activities Room,
she bites into a fig bar.

Three of her teeth come out.
She holds them up like gems

in the fluorescence,
considers each one,

lines them up on the table—
ivory, silver, gold—

goes back to coloring
without saying a word.

Accident Report

In the circle of wheelchairs,
I find my mother right away—
she's the one being spoon-fed

baked apples and ice cream
by an aide who exclaims,
Look who's here!

My mother looks up,
her blue eyes cornflowers
from a long-ago season.

She smiles out of muscle memory
or habit, or because it's expected,
or because she recognizes me—

a flicker of genetic code
still transmitting from the ether
of her consciousness somehow.

She grinds the teeth she still has
back and forth, back and forth.
I heard it from the doorway,

conditioned to it now, a sound
I could use to track her
if we were lost and wandering

in a moonless desert, which I guess
is where we are. Where she lives,

I am no longer the daughter,

and when I visit her there,
I know this to be true. Love
is a rolling code no one can decipher.

I think about these things—
about encrypted codes
and signal-tracking,

about who is and is not
still a mother, still a daughter—
about how I became a parent

not by carelessness or choice,
not even by immaculate conception,
but by virtue of plain bad luck:

a small silver car rolling like a dime
through an intersection where a red light
was not enough to stop a lumber truck,

and then ten years of an accident
still happening, still happening,
still happening.

What I Did on the 500th Day

On the 500th day of meditation,
I stood in the yard before sunrise,
saw the moon at rest in the nest of her halo.

I ate a speckled red apple with a tough skin,
threw the core in the woods for a squirrel.

I brushed the dog on the back deck,
watched her fur float away on cold air.
It was the winter of her sixteenth year.

I sat with my mom, who asked
if a scarf she had knitted was my boyfriend
and if she could marry my husband.

I said *yes* and *yes*.
It was a day to say yes.

I walked in the late afternoon,
a mile for every hundred days,
chanted a naming mantra

dirt   grass   mulch
pine cones   leaves   sand.

Reunion

my body, my mind, my soul & all my moms
　　are hanging around in the nursing home
　　the only place that can hold us all

i love you for me says dementia-mom

i see everything you do, kid says imaginary-mom
　　who always translates & only exists as a wish

so many lonely here says the orderly
　　who walked in when no one was looking
　　you have your angel wings for sure

an angel is just another fucked-up superhero
　　chants the chorus of knotted ligaments
　　where my wings should be

your mom is lucky to have you says dementia-mom
　　forgetting who she is

i was lucky to have her says my mind
　　regretting the past tense

the definition of happiness is gratitude
　　says real-mom from the long-ago

how long asks my soul
　　in the prison of gratitude?

here today, gone tomorrow!

says the child version of my mom
who likes to make light of my soul

not so fast i say out loud

all the moms laugh at the same time
& we are happier
than we have ever ever been

Infinity

I used to wish that when it was all over,
I'd be able to visit an alternate universe
where we'd be our true selves again: you
in your fifties, me visiting from college, my heart
years away from knowing what breaking was,
my arms resting on the cool Spanish tiles
while you made drinks. We'd go out to the patio,
dangle our feet in the double-hexagon pool,
a cubist infinity symbol, and I'd tell you the story
of how it all happened. I'd skip over the worst parts,
like how they tried to put you on antipsychotic drugs
because you went naked into the dining room
and it was upsetting to people who were visiting
their fully clothed parents. Instead, I'd start
with an abridged version of the car accident.
Then I'd tell you the funny things you said
when you started to go off the deep end.
I'd describe the pretty silver of your hair,
and tell you how everyone always loved you
no matter how crazy you became,
even if they didn't know you before.
Because you were always still you, somehow.
We'd have gin and tonics with triangles of lime,
and our glasses would sweat pleasantly
while our feet swayed back and forth
in the silky and luminous water. The lights
of Los Angeles would still obscure the stars,
but you would fill the universe around us
with your radiant face and your radiant eyes
and your radiant soul. You'd say how wonderful

this life is, no matter what. You'd tell me
I handled everything exactly right, just as you knew
I would. Later, we'd curl up on opposite ends
of the Danish sofa, where just by sitting together,
even with all that happened, we'd remember
how lucky we are. You'd get out your brushes
and your ink, and write in the air, in the calligraphy
of your unmistakable hand, *ad astra per aspera:*
to the stars, through difficulties

The Agnostic's Rapture

She goes out exactly as she would
have wanted: in the shimmering
warmth of morphine, swaddled
in snowy blankets

during an afternoon nap, two days
before Thanksgiving. No one else
is there. Her mouth had fallen open
the day before, gone slack

and stayed that way, no longer
the mouth that laughed and sang
and told me most of what
I would ever need to know.

After the body lets go, the soul
flows out the mouth and nose
the way a river splits around a rock,
rejoins itself to go on. The soul

swirls between bedrails, passes
through fabric someone wove
to make a privacy curtain long ago.
It leaves the room, goes down the hall,

past laundry bins and towering racks
of picked-over meal trays, gathers
like a cloud to wait for the elevator.
It rides one floor down, floats

into the lobby like an aroma—
in this case (but not always)
a pleasant one, like cookies
or birthday cake.

The woman working the desk
realizes how hungry she is,
so hungry she doesn't notice
when the glass doors glide open

and the soul shows itself out,
declares itself done with bricks
and steel, with non-slip mats
and parking lots, with freeways

and trees, with roofs on buildings
and vapor trails left by planes.
It hands over its few remaining
attachments, including me.

It leaves me to be anchored,
as she once was, by sleeping cats,
by blankets and loss, by the lack
of light in a room. It leaves me

to my breath, which does not belong
to me. Listen how it keeps choosing me
for its home. Listen how careful it is
to never make a single promise.

Aloha

I had a plan for her ashes. I would fly
to Oahu, where she spent *a glorious year*
after she left her doctor boyfriend
because he didn't like jazz, quit her job
at the hospital, and boarded the *SS Lurline*
to Honolulu. Not yet thirty, she did
as she pleased. I too would go barefoot,
climb into an outrigger canoe, paddle out
from Waikiki Beach. I would wear
her cowry-shell necklace, and someone
would play slack-key guitar. I'd float
a lei of yellow plumeria, the flower
that blooms even after its tree is uprooted.
I'd pour her ashes into the circle,
watch them glimmer down and disappear.
Later I'd go to The Royal Hawaiian,
which used to be known as the *pink palace*
of the Pacific. I'd sit at a table facing the ocean,
have a drink, think about how she returned
with me a decade later. I was eight then.
How we loved the Hawaiian men,
with their soft voices and their soft hands,
their offerings of pineapple in the morning,
guava juice in the afternoon. I decide
I will write a note, roll it up like a scroll,
seal it with cork into a seaworthy bottle,
to tell the pineapple-guava men
we are coming back. I just don't know when.

A Daughter Is Clearing Out the House Next Door

I have done this. I know how it is to enter a life
not your own, yet one so known it could be.

To see everything saved, only to be abandoned
this way. Left-behind books. Sweater on a hook.

Carved wooden box with a tuft of cat fur inside.
Towels folded in a narrow closet. Basement full

of broken tools. Kitchen full of cooking pots.
Chocolate bar among the cups. To face

the evidence of unpaid bills, forgotten pills,
colonoscopy photos in a take-out menu,

forty-seven shoehorns—one in the pantry.
To drive to the landfill and the charity store

until you barely feel it anymore.
Next-door daughter, you will be all right.

Work into the night if you want to survive.
Look for something to leave behind.

Shells in a line on a windowsill.
An emerald bottle to catch the light.

When it was my time, I walked to the creek,
found a palm-sized rock to leave on the porch,

my mark on the canvas of this time.
Wayfinder, relic, message, mudra—

the tumbled-smooth gray they call *river stone*—
is black ash when it rains, a dove in the sun.

Four

Saturation

The people have gone inside,
left their shoes tangled like kelp
at every door, their towels draped
like ghosts of those lost at sea,

this absence a gift to skunks
who drift across lawns, pixelating
in and out of shadows, a slow
procession of black and white

that draws all color from cosmos
and marigold in a charcoal vapor
and summons the shape-shifting hour,
when everything becomes anything

and the world seems so full of meaning
it might have no meaning at all.

Synapse

I smelled her before I saw her
and my brain said *deer*
around the same time her brain
probably said *human* and *run*
and it was not until two seconds later
when she burst out of the woods
already bouncing up the trail
waving the crisp white handkerchief
of her tail   that my eyes relayed
the rest of it to my conscious mind.
I was two legs and a startle response,
she was four legs and a shot of fear,
yet she sailed through the undergrowth
and leaf litter without a sound.
I saw her again as I came over the rise.
She had paused on the path
to look my way. I'd like to think
she was as interested in me
as I was in her, but I know
she was calculating *safety*
versus *danger:* the coordinates
of where she stood
plus the amount of time
she would need to stay away
from the fawn folded into a bed
of pine needles and brittle leaves
minus the rate I was moving
in the right direction (*away*).
I miss the world
the way it almost used to be.

Naïve Melody

one round of the sound
of a great horned owl
in winter light

the notes unfurl like wings
and fold into silence

and though I know she stopped
because she heard me

I stay where I am
because I heard her too

so we listen together
one of us waiting for presence
the other for absence

my gift to her
is to go on

Extra Terrestrial

The toad emerges dry and yellow-green
after days of heat and dust, wedges out
from under clumps of mulch in the beds.
I oblige and water him. He pushes up
on bulldog arms and slits his eyes
against my rain. The more I water,
the darker he gets, the earthy olive-grey
a toad ought to be. I move on
to the hydrangeas, but I keep him
in my sight. From across the yard,
I admire his muscleman shoulders
and bandy legs, the neckless continuum
of his body, the razor stripe of white
that splits the warty landscape of his back.
I roll the hose and go back to him, kneel
and slip the pad of my finger under his palm.
What am I to a convex eye that mirrors
like a garden orb? I imagine the bones
inside his bony fingers, the pulse
of his blood, the poison gland
behind each postorbital ridge.
He tolerates me, expressionless.

Feral Muse

He sits ill-tempered in a slash of sun
that angles the driveway, or reclines defiant
on the trailer's steely wishbone. At dusk
he scales the fence to lurk beneath shrubs

while I'm out with the dog, as if he knows
she's gone deaf and blind and he can gloat at last.
One night I looked out at the first falling snow,
saw his surly shape glaring at the screen door.

His fur was as dull as he was sour, his ratty coat
the color of damp dirt. I thought I could let him
onto the porch, at least, if not out of the cold.
But he flattened and hissed as I opened the latch,

and looked back with contempt as he slunk away
with an unfinished poem in his mouth.

Rabbit in a Rainstorm

a rabbit has taken refuge
under the front porch
because the rain comes in torrents
for days these days
and it is all too much
for anyone's fur to repel

especially if you were born
with a brain that takes everything in
no time to sift or decide what's a threat
and what is not   at a certain point
it's a trip-wire to survive
which means you freeze
or you run or you hide

so we sit   kindred
waiting for the rain to let up
one of us in the dimming above
the other in near-darkness below
both surrounded by our comforts

mine a burled tree root I carried
from the destroyed forest
when nothing else could be saved

a thin wooden buddha
standing mute in the corner

my mother's wicker chair
unwinding at the edges

a string of lantern lights that sags
but holds the line

the rabbit in her shallow nest
scratched into dry dirt and dead leaves

settling into a stillness   where light
the same as mine

spills between floorboards
in thin stripes across her damp fur

More

Enough is abundance to the wise. —Euripides

I have little to offer the forest today
except not burning   not marking
not cutting or killing or harming

but I know enough to be grateful
for the familiar brutality
of icy wind off the lake

for the trees that protect me from it
even dead they offer handholds
for the climb up   a weathered railing
for the way down

the trees are not here for me
but I thank them anyway

and if gratitude begins with attention
all I have to do is notice
the fiery carpet of sunlit needles
on a spiral stairway of trail

all I have to do is listen
to the percussion of my boots
on roots   to know
I walk on hollowed ground

the genius work
of denning snake mothers
whose blunt faces
push everything aside

Walking a Dog for a Friend Who Is Away

We agreed that he would lead, being familiar
with the neighborhood. I followed, tethered

by a neon yellow leash that matched his harness.
We turned away from the poisonous noise

of blowers and mowers, moved briskly
past yards with signs that signaled bigotry

or proclaimed the lack of it. The tail of a squirrel,
dead from collision, waved from the street,

lifted by the breeze. We left the sidewalk
for a grassy hill covered with pine cones,

skirted the fence of an aging tennis court,
and assessed two picnic tables, found them

no worse for winter. It was spring. We were surprised
by a rabbit. We visited the places where dogs

leave messages, and he read each one
with thoughtful attention. I have only 6 million

to his 300 million smell receptors, and I lack
the nostril flaps to hold molecules in,

so there's no hope I'll ever learn the language.
Some messages required careful analysis.

There was gender to consider, and social status,

and whether the author was known or a stranger.

He added to each conversation. But as we went on,
his comments grew cursory, like a bureaucrat

initialing papers he can't be bothered to read.
I wasn't sure if he was losing interest

or if his pen was running dry. I didn't bring up
the families, four of them, who brought him

back to the shelter without a fair trial,
or all the dogs who run out of time and luck

every day of the year. Everyone loves a puppy,
not so much the emerging dog. Instead,

we inspected the park next to the library,
which was closed. Fast-food wrappers

and nip bottles were scattered about, despite
a conveniently placed bin. He waited politely

as I gathered my disappointments and put them
where they belonged. We crossed the ballfield

to clear our minds, and headed for the lake
to look for turtles on our way home.

Understudy

I became an assassin to save my black dog,
who arrived in my life with a universe of fears.

A fly in the house was one of the worst—
tucked tail, frantic eyes, an under-table dive

or zero-traction scramble for anywhere to hide.
Yet outside, flying insects were nothing to her.

Turns out it was the magazine's *smack*
she feared, the fly a predictor—

what happened before might happen again.
So I trained myself to listen, to stalk,

wadded tissue in hand, and crush each fly
in its fatal pause. Sixteen years on,

the black dog is gone, and now there's a cat
whose genes flipped a switch

that made her blind. But the cat does not care.
Ears pivot, whiskers quiver—she's all in

for the kill. Up the stairs, down the stairs,
a vertical launch, a faultless vault

over the table set for dinner. She plots
the coordinates of tables and chairs,

sensing and tracking whatever moves air,
adding it all to the map of unseen things

in a universe that is hers to define,
mine to learn how to trust.

Mouse Log

Scavenging firewood between storms, we find a pile
of unsplit oak the town left behind. The chipper
will be here tomorrow. I use my foot to push aside
a log almost too rotted to take, roll it toward our truck
anyway—until I see a white-footed mouse
tucked in one of its grooves, black eyes all pupil
as she tries to decide whether to jump or stay.
She backs in further, out of sight. So we lift the trunk
like a treasure, nestle it like fine sculpture in a corner
of the truck bed. At home, we unload the mouse log,
carry it like medics bearing a stretcher, and set it down
between two arbor vitae, a name that means *tree of life*,
a kind of tree we have in our yard, but also a structure
we carry in our cerebellum, a word that means *little brain*.
We have mice in our walls. No one can tell us how
to get them out alive before closing up the holes.
When I can't sleep, I think of the log-mouse
in her wooden burrow, the arbor vitae deep within
her cerebellum. When she dies, I hope she falls
to weather, to age, to tooth or claw. Not poison,
not a trap, not the chipper's screaming maw.

Five

Triangle

During the AIDS epidemic, San Francisco SPCA volunteers and their pets visited hospitals throughout the city.

By then I had been to the memorial quilt
laid out in the vast caverns of Moscone Center,
its glittery panels festooned with rainbows,

pink triangles, fancy fringed cowboy shirts,
tiaras, even a magic wand with streamers
and a star. People walked the edges

in a wobbly procession, reading names,
holding themselves, being held,
while boxes of tissues sat in the shadows

like chaplains with little to offer. By then
I had seen the young men, gaunt and weary,
as they rode the train to the Sunset District.

They gazed at the floor or out the windows
as lights came on, lovers found each other,
friends walked arm in arm to dinner.

But it wasn't for them I went to the hospital.
I went for anyone who might be there. I went
where they sent me, because I was weary

in a different way, and because I had a cat
named Butch, benevolent and fat, perfect
for the job. The nurse glanced up the hall

and led us to a locked ward. Nurses know
when doctors are out on rounds or napping
in the lounge. Nurses know what risk is

and what it is not. You don't worry
about toxoplasmosis when hope is gone.
She left us in a room where a man lay

motionless on his back, his dark hair
boyish, his eyes clear, his smile frozen
yet radiant. His hands were as flat and stiff

as gloves lost to a storm, the bones
of his body a topographical map.
Butch squeezed through the bedrails,

settled his massive body against the frail one.
The man lifted his arms, skimmed his palms
over Butch's fur. Between the ears. Down

the neck. Along the back. Over, over,
over. He never spoke, never took his eyes
away from mine. If you want to know

what I remember most about that time,
it would be that room: the three of us
ephemeral, eternal, holding each other,

being held in the incandescent emptiness
of the pink triangle I still carry.

Ikebana in the Hospital

So much to take in as I wait on my gurney.
I focus on my breath.

Cool air in. Warm air out.
The kindness of my nurse, her voice

a curly willow. The way she compliments the vein
on the back of my hand, inserts the needle.

The old woman on the next gurney
telling her nurse about the death of her husband,

her insomnia. The quietness of her crying.
I want to sweep aside the privacy curtain,

hold her hand while we wait.
Instead, I close my eyes, send *metta*

through the thin fabric. *May she be safe.*
May she be well. May she be peaceful.

The anesthesiologist arrives bearing oxygen,
a colorless branch with two out-of-season buds.

I accept. I do. I breathe.

The Meeting of Habit and Grief

After we climb the stairs
and fall into sleep, and the only
remaining dog curls into her bed,
your father reads in the aura
of a single lamp, half-glasses
just below the bridge of his nose.
In this late solitude, his habit
is to set the book aside,
shamble off to the kitchen,
rummage the cupboards
for chocolate. But tonight
he's been dead for three days,
so he just sits, a ghost with his book
in his old hands, and reads.

When daylight bleeds in
at the edges, we come downstairs.
We think we see a familiar indent
in the cushion of the big chair.
So we go around the creaky spots
on the floor, trying not to wake him.
But then we remember that today
our bones ache, and the dog
has to be carried to the yard,
and even though there are dark-
red strawberries for breakfast,
in our mouths they will taste
like dust.

My Father-in-Law Arrives for the Last Time

A week to the day after you died,
here you are on the front porch
in a postal carton—as much of a surprise

as if you'd arrived unannounced
in your bucket hat and tattered red jacket,
your hair unruly with age, crooked hand

clutching a jar of marmalade. Always
the same gift, though you were the only one
who ate it. And here I am, not-quite-daughter,

the only one home to take you in, surprised
by the heft of what is left of you, a boisterous,
blustery life already converted to stills:

journeys to libraries, to symphony halls,
to museums and monuments—the Oracle
at Delphi, for heaven's sake. Grand cathedral

or humble church, your voice like thunder
in pew or pulpit, which was anywhere
you were. Even in our house,

you'd pound the table to make a point,
never mind that it scared the dog. All this
in a box too small for all you were,

yet much too heavy for the frailty of last year—
legs like twigs, skin gone thin, bright eyes
of a bird. But you walked and walked

and walked the city, even on the last day,
when you strode into the June sunlight,
lungs alive with morning-glorious air—

setting off for the arboretum
and the end of your life, which came
as a blinding sizzle and pop,

like the flash of an old-time camera,
and under the dark cloth, the photographer:
your god.

Trompe l'oeil on the Capital Beltway

The clouds today are biblical, towering,
a painted mountain range you can imagine
Moses running down, robes aflutter, stone
tablets flung open like shutters. Everyone
slows down. We try to keep our eyes
on the road, but we're drawn to the false
ceiling of the sky, as if our cars could rise,
disappear into all this glory, so many grains
of salt and sand. And I think I understand
why some look for divinity on high,
and miss so much of the grounded world—
two slugs in a yin-yang mating curl, a beetle
who clings to a swaying blade of grass.

If I'm Lucky

the worst thing about dying will be
how I won't be able to write about it

what I thought & felt
what I saw & smelt

the *oh fuck!* or *what the hell…?* of it
or the last contented breath of it

the regret or peace or relief of it
the whack or languid pull of it

the radiance or dimming or fire of it
the antiseptic or floral rot of it

the simple unraveling
or sensory overload of it—

how I won't reveal if a colossal face
peers down through a hole in the clouds

if a massive hand scoops me up
like a cosmic Ferris wheel

& sets me back down as Cleopatra
or a dung beetle   or crushes me

in a divine comment on insignificance.

Native Daughter

Even though I never knew them, I think
about the Norwegian ladies who stood
behind tables piled with lefse at the church fair.
I imagine their side-eye, hear their hushed voices:
Charlotte's aren't what you'd call round,
but she's young yet.... And Hedvig's! Well,
she's been awful distracted by that fancy fella
from Saint Paul. Mabel Amanda's not one
to show pride, but aren't hers as delicate
as a lace curtain and round as the Wolf Moon.

And even though my mother was a black sheep
who sang in the choir before she ran off to the city,
and though I've never been one for church myself
(except with the grandparents on Easter—
The Affliction of the Patent-Leather Shoes),
and though it would come as no surprise that I too
ended up far from Minnesota, I think

the Norwegian ladies would recognize in me
a certain decisiveness with the notched rolling pin
and the turning stick. They'd notice how I never
let the dough make a trouble spot on the pastry cloth,
how I never have to measure the amount of flour
for the dredger.

The Norwegian church ladies are long gone,
but I can see them in all their plainness and glory,
looking down from their very own heaven.
They nod and smile, and though I only make lefse

once a year, they call me a *native daughter.*
Because from the celestial vantage point,
the lineage is as clear as wolf tracks in snow,
and they know my grandmother turned her lefse
with the stick from a roll-up window shade,
and afterward she washed it, dried it,
put it back for next time.

Mooncake in a Chinese Bakery

you came for this round wonder
on a paper plate

& found windows steamed
to invisibility

tables & chairs so close
you have to go sideways

to get the one seat left
at a rickety table by the wall

the bell on the door
an insistent message

from the world of the sidewalk
where gutters gutter over

& rain rains down
which you blissfully ignore

because you want to drown
in the refuge of voices

not one word you understand

not one face you know

not a soul who knows you

this happiness a measure
for all happiness

a lotus mooncake
the least of it

The Hawk Elizabeth

When the hawk swept in
to light on the juniper
an arm's length from me
and did not move,
I knew it was you.
I flashed back
to how we met—
strangers among strangers
in the crowded room
where you read your poem
about a phone call
to inform you of a death,
and you set the receiver
back in its cradle, twirled
and danced around
your living room.
I think you even sang.
You spoke your ecstasy
out loud, no explanation
but *fear nothing life brings—*
rise up to meet it.
You, a green shoot
of survival
from the dark soil
of the underworld
we shared. You,
a flare sent up
to embrace everything
unafraid. Even today,
the way you flew in

to say hello, the only
word you would use
as you got old.
Never goodbye.
Angel with talons
and a razor mouth,
you sweep open
the grand doorway
of the sky, your blue
going-blind eyes
lit, lit, lit.

Science & Religion @ 5 am

would never have seen her
if I hadn't heard a screech owl
hadn't stopped in the still-
dark street   hadn't

turned around   (how
senseless   to look for an owl
or try to unravel the mystery
of what in us   turns & turns

toward what can never be known
or known again)   a streetlamp
could not be less of a mystery
yet it too was essential   light & hinge

to open the way for the gift:
black outline of wolf   emerging
from the ancient cemetery
a black pause in the pale flicker

I am a believer in the genome:
its continuity across & within species
how it blurs distinctions
between ancestor   descendant

& living being   so I knew
she was there: guardian
spirit animal   my wolfish dog
dead three years   yet steadfast

both of us   inside the summoning
of a bell only we could hear
it was the morning of my birthday
& all day I carried the gift:

knowing she had paused in the pitch-
black shadows between headstones
watched as I walked by   waited
& calculated a perfect arc

over the black iron fence
into the intersection of our worlds
to make of them   one world
before she crossed the street   away

Personal Acknowledgments

My deepest gratitude to all who helped bring this book into being:

Hank Hudepohl and everyone at Pine Row Press, for believing in the power of poetry.

my teachers and friends in the poetry universe, for the astonishing generosity, dedication, and beauty they bring into the world: Ellen Bass, Susan Berlin, John Bonanni, Polly Brody, Mary E. Cronin, Nancy Cherico, Mark Doty, Patty Enrado, Barbara Fried, Margo Greenhow, Alice Kociemba, Dorianne Laux, Merryn Rutledge, Donna Scheer, Ruby Shifrin, and Lauren Wolk.

Alisa Backer Jaskiewicz, who knows the stories behind the stories behind the stories.

John Strong Parke, who somehow manages to be both the rock in the middle of the churning river and the water that flows around all obstacles.

my parents, always with me, even now.

the dogs and cats who came bearing wisdom, inspiration, and occasional dead things: Addie, Butch, Muffy, Helen, Jimmy, Pearl, Sam, Saturn, Scooter, Smitty, Toshi, and Vera.

the wild inhabitants of water, land, and sky, for sharing glimpses of their lives and saving mine.

About the Author

Brett Warren (she/her) is an editor who holds a BA in English literature from the University of California, Santa Barbara. Her poetry has appeared in *Cape Cod Poetry Review, Canary, The Comstock Review, Halfway Down the Stairs, Harbor Review, Hole in the Head Review,* and many other publications. She lives in Massachusetts, in a house surrounded by pitch pine and black oak trees—nighttime roosts of wild turkeys, who sometimes use the roof of her writing attic as a runway.

More at brettwarrenpoetry.com

Made in the USA
Columbia, SC
15 February 2023

12442645R00067